MW00812714

Woodworking for Kids

The Ultimate Guide to Teach Your Children About Woodworking + Innovative DIY Projects

EDDIE BLAKE

This document is geared towards providing exact and reliable information in regards to the topic and issue covered. The publication is sold with the idea that the publisher is not required to render accounting, officially permitted, or otherwise, qualified services. If advice is necessary, legal or professional, a practiced individual in the profession should be ordered.

guarantee assurance. The trademarks that are used are without any consent, and the publication of the trademark is without permission or backing by the trademark owner. All trademarks and brands within this book are for clarifying purposes only and are the owned by the owners themselves, not affiliated with this document.

Table of Contents

Introduction

The importance of woodworking in early childhood education was acknowledged after the fabulous and unique contributory work of Friedrich Froebel. He believed that children who studied using both their hands and minds were expected to exhibit more interest and involvement in their studies than children who were denied such facilities and activities. Froebel stressed allowing children constructive participation in realistic thinking. He strongly recommended incorporating creative elements in physical activities during simple day-to-day tasks and pursuit of passions.

There is no convincing evidence that Froebel himself specifically made arrangements for woodwork activities under his kindergarten arrangement. Still, it was soon accepted as an additional activity when Froebel's kindergarten concepts spread across the globe. In his former school in Keilhau, Froebel initiated woodwork for older children and included them in several major building ventures at the farm.

Froebel's teachings emphasized playing and learning through connection with natural materials and experiences with nature, which he saw as both nourishing for the soul

and essential for the holistic development of the children.

The influence of Froebel's work spread internationally through the Sloyd education movement. In Uno Cygnaeus, Finland (1810–1888) was inspired by Froebel's ideas, and in 1866 it became compulsory to introduce craftwork into folk schools through his work. Cygnaeus intended to create the children's hands-on practical knowledge and talents, aesthetic idea, and through the craft, method developed children's thinking. He got his work In Froebel's kindergarten as a natural development. Sloyd attempted to gain functional experience, solve practical challenges through knowledge of multiple operating processes, and learn how to analyze and optimize work through experimentation. The woodwork was at the forefront but included other crafts like folding paper and working with fabrics. It was assumed that working with hands would increase cognitive development and make learning more relevant, building confidence, and instilling respect for labor dignity. The ideas of Froebel and those of the Sloyd movement together inspired the introduction of woodworking in the

UK and many other countries. Implementation was tailored in reaction to the current tool types and established techniques. It culminated in somewhat different country-to-country approaches to woodwork though maintaining a transparent traditional core.

With the development of the global economy, woodwork lost popularity in the 50s and 60s, made it seen as 'old fashioned, and was found more appropriate for less academic children. Today we are starting to see a shifting trend of nursery environments and classrooms – originating with the early childhood market. There's a noisy revolution! It's great to know that interest growing and renewed. The prevailing thought is that children need opportunities to experience risk and learn to assess self-risk rather than being protected and covered in cotton wool. Kids must learn to make decisions and judgments so they can defend themselves better in new situations. Froebel's ideas are once again being embraced. There is growing awareness in woodworking and the establishment of training stations in childhood settings.

Chapter 1: Understanding the Importance of Woodworking for Young Children

Woodworking is a challenging and exciting activity, and it contributes to the disciplined growth and grooming of children in a competitive environment. Woodwork encompasses play and creativity as central elements of development and learning integration. Woodwork involves developing the 'whole' child care arrangements and, in particular, well-being and trust. It gives children a sense of agency as they work with their hands, heart, and minds, a 'can-do' spirit that develops as they put their ideas into action.

Playing and experiencing open-ended natural resources is essential to healthy development. Woodwork provides material for children to play, explore, and express their imagination in a convincing style. Children learn to work and play with tools. It helps them to acquire the first-hand experience while involved in creating something new. This undeterred exploration of materials leads to more profound kinds of learning achieved through play.

Woodwork provides interaction with wood's natural material, connecting children to the natural world and building sensitivity to the material. Learning with woodwork is meaningful and relates to the interests and experiences of the children. Wood's smell and feel, using real tools, working with natural material, hammering and sawing sounds, hands and minds working together to express their imagination and solve problems, using strength and coordination: all go together to captivate the interest of young children. Woodwork assists in the development of:

Woodworking is a common hobby for particularly parents and kids, who can jointly carry out activities. Parents and kids can collaborate toward a project-based task, generate memories and quick interactions through the procedure of creating something from beginning to end, and several suggested newbie wood crafts can be customized for children to enjoy their free time. Woodwork is a great tool for imaginative artwork and innovative designs. It also has the advantage of encompassing several other fields of learning and advancement to include a genuinely cross-curricular experience. Numerical reasoning is being developed, analytical expertise is being acquired, technical awareness is being established through experimenting with equipment, and kids becoming engineers while they show. Woodwork is phenomenal for improving children's imaginative and analytical thinking abilities. Children tweak and play with the combinations of wood and equipment and then communicate thoughts and solve the tasks. But woodwork is not all about what kids do – it's more about the adjustments that occur within the kid. Woodwork has a significant effect on a kid's personality and confidence and provides a spirit of agency. Woodwork is a way for kids to show their imagination and ingenuity. It is necessary not to develop projects in which all kids generate a similar object. The key to children staying very interested in woodwork is that they pursue their desires and address their issues to build their task. When it has been started and is guided by kids, all discoveries appear more valuable. Children learn at their natural speed of woodwork and experience their difficulties. When they have learned practical techniques, they step through clean experimentation, exploring opportunities, and then producing creative inventions. Since kids pursue their targets to do what they like to do, they have the innate desire to survive and improve from failures to fix problems. When they face and overcome new tasks, their creativity, innovative thought, and problem-solving capabilities develop. It is incredible to see exactly how much training in a woodworking exercise is included. It includes all fields of growth, promoting optimistic, imaginative kids with a desire for lifelong activity. Mathematical reasoning, science study, technical information advancement, a greater understanding of the surroundings, physiological growth and synchronization, communication and speech, and social and emotional development are mixed into woodworking

- Children to create the connection between awareness of daily life and beauty

- Appreciation of the natural world's beauty/respect for nature/tree knowledge/sustainability

- Awareness that we should produce and restore – establish an organization – and the value of building and repairing rather than using and disposing of money

- Authentic first-hand experiences – real-world instruments/materials

- Experience the beauty, knowledge, and life forms

1.1 Benefits of Woodworking for Children

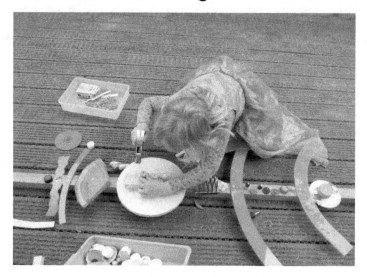

Listed below are the advantages and benefits of woodworking for children:

Freedom

It gives them freedom and liberty to create and build objects of their choice.

Woodwork should be open-ended to allow children to play a leading role in their learning. Children will make their own choices and decisions at the center. They will continuously develop skills, and building on past knowledge, and woodwork offers plenty of opportunity for rich multi-layered progress. Free choice and self-activity with guidance from the adult are important Froebelian concepts.

- Woodwork draws curiosity – the inquiry spirit

- Gives the first-hand experience

- Builds upon inherent motivation

- Engagement sustained-no time limits-flow

- Child selections initiated-and option becomes part of continuous provision

- Risk-taking under managed conditions/self-treatment

- Feeling confident and respected / use of tools

- Graduated challenge – with wood/tools – progression as skill and trust

- Opportunity to fix issues in their jobs, time, and energy

Guidance

Clearly, with woodwork, we need to guide the kids on how to use the tools safely and nurture their critical and creative thinking skills as they solve problems to solve their job.

- Respect for children seen as healthy learners

- Introduction of the instruments and techniques

- Respect for the materials and tools

- Safety, hazards, and risks emphasized and discussed

- Ensure safe use continued

- Being offered as an extra hand

- Reciprocal relationship-the teacher resonating

- Interacting when it's useful to extend your thinking – open-ended questions / remember previous questions

- Expertise

- To facilitate reflection and assessment, and to share with

  others

- Suggest other dynamics – for instance, paper to express initial ideas

- Constant vision area-in-line overview

- Structural freedom – balance to allow for rich explorations

- Emphasis on unfinished commodity processes

- Individual and the community

- Choice of ergonomic tools and softwoods to help you learn independently

- Projects grouped to facilitate communication and collaboration

- Humility and respect

- Share the ideas and thoughts with others

- Reflect on their mutual work

Observation

Several instances of schematic duplication frequently arise at the workbench that allows children to repeat and gain trust and security. The statement helps adults see what kids are doing and act in light of these observations. It may help what the child is doing, or the child could enjoy the continuation of the learning. Life at the woodwork bench offers rich opportunities for practitioners to immensely observe development and education as children shape their thinking skills.

Inner/ Outer

Wood provides another material for expressing imagination and emotion in this way, 'making' the inner-outer. Wood

and tools arouse children's interest and curiosity and stimulate them to express their inner thoughts. It's a particular mode of speech – mixing architecture with materials and working in three dimensions. The outer making process stimulates children to develop new inner feelings, create ideas and narratives, questions and solutions, and foster satisfaction and well-being. The external forces and sensations are internal.

Environment and movement

With woodwork presenting children with the most suitable tools and materials optimal for their current level of development, it is important not to introduce frustration but to build confidence and competence. For young learners, movement is imperative, and woodwork is so rich in many aspects of physical development, such as fine skills, gross motor skills, hand-eye coordination, and self-care, etc.

The whole child, Unity, and Expression

Creativity nourishes the essence of man-it elevates our souls, and transcends the earthly world. Human beings are fundamentally successful and imaginative, and by cultivating these following the universe comes fulfillment. We need to encourage the creation of educational environments that involve practical work and direct material utilization. Learning unfolds by interacting with the universe. Play is an imaginative practice, and with it, children are aware of their role in the universe. By developing creativity, children are allowed to play, express their imagination, and represent symbolically. They can connect and explore ideas, thoughts, and feelings.

Woodwork is a hard material to work with. It provides constant problems – it is extraordinary how powerful it is to develop children's creative and critical thinking as they solve problems and express their imagination. They develop perseverance when they deal with resources and strive to produce the performance they desire. Woodworking fosters freedom, and as children are accustomed to addressing challenges that occur through their playing, they feel secure in their abilities to solve concerns when they emerge.

Only children can learn what they are prepared for. Children are developing differently and should be allowed to learn at their own pace of development. By holding the woodwork available to them, the developmental stage that is correct for them will naturally gravitate – be it unpressed experimentation, pursuing their fascinations, structural repetition, or creation with a purpose in mind (representative, abstract/story, etc.). Other advantages are:

The Knowledge Forms

- Information sources are interconnected and work alongside different types

- Knowledge of timber as material, properties, trees, wood use

- Expertise in tools and techniques

- Computer skills and abstract reasoning

- The knowledge and understanding of science

- Learning how to make and repair, instead of consuming and disposing

- An account of technology

- Designing thought processes

Gifts to Occupations

There is a natural progression from contributing to the occupations-from playing wooden blocks to building with wood-playing with risks. Children handle things with care, and they take great pride in their achievements through rising mastery, accuracy, and challenge solving. But always remember woodwork isn't about what kids do – what is made in woodwork gives new neural pathways as kids develop confidence, self-esteem, creative and critical thinking skills, mathematical problem-solving skills, etc. At the woodwork bench, you can see children growing taller!

Beginning of a Noisy Revolution

As kids make wood, they learn skills that will encourage them to make their world. Today, most children in most of the world's developed countries will have no experience working with real tools in all of their education. It is a disservice for children because many occupations involve the usage of equipment skillfully. It is rarely found in elementary schools, and most schools avoid working with rigid materials. The government stresses the need for more pupils to go into the research, production, architecture, and creativity industries. It left many kids with no understanding to work with tools at all in their entire education. It is wrong with kids, and many refused this chance unless they are lucky enough to gain these services at home. Many children will need practical skills to work as scientists, plumbers, electricians, technicians, carpenters, dentists, mechanics, builders, etc. There is an extensive range of occupations in which the skill to be professional with equipment plays a significant role, from the development of electronics and technology projects to surgical tools in surgery or dental practice. Some universities have recently published articles about intelligent students who lack the practical skills to build a basis for theory related to subjects like engineering, science, and product design. Functional tooling abilities are also beneficial to us in our everyday lives, whether it's performing DIY procedures, indulging in a hobby, or making fixes.

We are now starting to look at the changing landscape of nursery in classrooms, reception, and schools – originating with the early childhood market. There's a noisy transformation! It is heartening to watch this new and rising interest marvelously. The concept of young kids working with tools surprises many. Woodwork, fortunately, has a strong history of childhood education dating back to the mid-1800s. Still, the woodwork was almost entirely eradicated in the '80s and '90s with the burdensome atmosphere of risk prevention and over-zealous protection worries exacerbated by the litigation environment. The current prevailing thought is that kids need exposure to experience risk to assess self-risk rather than being over-protected and covered in a cotton ball. It had almost vanished in recent decades, but now it is making a return, with revived enthusiasm from several colleges. In early childhood surroundings and primary schools, there's a dire need to promote woodwork. Children should be able to obtain from the rich woodworking opportunities it offers. Working with wood can be very empowering for kids.

The Growth

He needs to engage his brain a little while a kid deals with wood to visualize; when they tackle the issues, he encounters something when creating things. He performs and learns to remove errors. The development of answers to the project's challenges allows kids to learn strategies that they can utilize in their infancy and build these abilities into youth.

Creativeness

The creativity of woodworking projects goes side by side. In general, people familiar with dealing with wood are more inventive because they have to create fresh, practical items out of simple wood and deal with several problems relating to carpentry. Working with wood is also an apt activity for children who, as contrasted to adults, have more significant room to develop (both mentally and physically).

You cannot merely obtain designs that have been created

with mission and vision in sight, but kids who are skilled in woodworking can start making their designs, creations, and bringing to existence their innovative ideas.

Growth in physical form

Let's admit it is part of most kids' upbringing nowadays, and there is a lot of screen time. It can be challenging to identify ways children can get involved and to be creative about it. Woodworking allows to physically promote growth, as it can be challenging to operate with the massive tools and materials needed to execute woodworking ventures.

Teamwork Allows the Dream Work

Woodworking is not only a solitary activity but may even be carried out in teams. With the support of their peers, parents should encourage their kids to do a larger project. It will enable them to peacefully coexist and understand each other, which will increase confidence and respect for each other. It is often a chance for parents to come closer to their kids, or through working jointly on woodworking ventures, siblings can become connected.

Keep it healthy

Kids will have a good time creating creative stuff, placing in the physical work, and get the most fundamental value

of a hobby, the feeling of accomplishment you get after staring at the "piece of art" you made. As a dad, you can have a life full of meaningful experiences, items made with your hands.

This hobby's result is not a compilation intended to be put on the racks but an everyday use item. It is also not a waste of time, hard work, and resources, contrary to collection activities. Again, he/she can do it as a proper career if the child has any average compatibility, as it is instead a successful job.

The communication and development of languages

There is still a lot of debate on the work desk, and terminology is also established. Children have to obey directions, and other children can even be heard discussing the rules and regulations. Most of the time, they face challenges and discuss strategies. They describe what they perform and acquire the language relevant to the task.

Advancement in mathematics

From witnessing the wood's weight and scale to determining how many wheels to fit a vehicle, this permeates every part of the job. Kids are going to focus on shape and size, as well as quantity. Also, their ideas may be conveyed, improved, and founded with suitable interaction.

Development of literacy

Kids may sometimes merge mark-making to woodwork - trying to add to their designs drawn functionalities. They also include a name to guarantee that their task is not ruined. For ideas or facts, they will utilize books to relate to. As described above, several models would also be used in stories, and there are endless opportunities for literacy within it.

Awareness of the World

They can explore how to utilize tools and how to mix various materials. They may gain knowledge about the origins of wood and different kinds of wood with sufficient experience. They're likely to undergo the 'plan, create, evaluate' stage.

Chapter 2: Woodworking Tools for Kids

Having the most appropriate tools makes a huge difference and can reduce risk. The primary tools used for woodworking are:

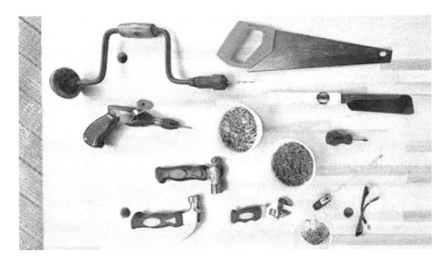

2.1 Hammer

The best hammer is a ball-pein hammer, which is "stubby." These are all easily accessible now. They are designed to hammer out in awkward places for adults, but they are a perfect weight for young children. They have small handles, so they are more controllable and have a wide hitting surface, making the nail easier.

2.1 Saw

Small children saws that cut on the pull stroke are much simpler to use, more controllable and need less energy. These days there are several pull-saws available in the market. Advice is to go for Japanese pull saws-they are small, they have thin edges, and everyone who uses them is taken aback by how simple it is to use them. These are used to hold the handle with both hands.

2.2 Hand-drill

The safest hand drills are those with enclosed mechanisms, as there is minimal

risk of fingers getting trapped in the uncovered cogs. Ensure the work is clamped while drilling. Small drill-bits will not snap frequently.

2.3 Screwdriver

Use a stubby screwdriver. It is easy to operate a short-handled screwdriver, and the "cross" design ensures that the screwdriver is less likely to slip out of the screw.

Early in their life, it's essential to instill a work ethic in their youth, but it's equally necessary to show them how to love learning and learn different skills, and it all begins at home. Kids will still recall the first collection of devices that they put their hands on, which they know. Yet where should you continue with all the instruments out there?

2.4 Ratchet and Wrench Set

Bicycles may just be the kid's link to the real world. Yet beyond that, they are a gateway to great exploration about how things function. The dismantling of excellent bikes gives a peek beneath the plastic veneer. The keys to disassembling and reassembling are ratchet and wrench. This ratchet and wrench package is perfect for disassembling items and bringing them back together.

2.5 Bench Vise

If you choose to transform a wooden block into something more, you should be showing your child how to work on a desk. You will need a 4-inches jaw spread, the heavy-duty woodworking vise, along an anvil to help you whack everything into place. You can use this for anything from home welding and steel cutting to bar stock clamping. A swivel base is installed; the built-in pipe clamp is calibrated for working round stock.

2.6 Measuring Tape

Tape measures are sweet tools for kids. Tape measures are additionally essential tools around the house. You can use it to teach your child numbers and then fractions. The measuring tape above should be about right for children. Small hands can reach the lock, and the blade extends a useful distance for small projects and play.

Have two Panel Saws: Cross and Rip-Cut

Handsaws (also called "panel saws") are large, slim saws with a sturdy wooden handle. They are used to scale the lumber. A panel saw is a smaller handsaw that matches into the board of a tool chest. Panel saws are available in two tooth configurations. You are going to need both:

Rip-Cut

It cuts down the grain like a chisel.

2.7 Cross-Cut

- It cuts down the grain like a knife.

- Panel saws are affordable. However, you need to know what you're looking for exactly. Moreover, you must be able to spend some time practicing how to sharpen hand saws.

- Measure Twice, Cut Once

- The importance of double-checking your measurements really can't be stressed enough. Having to start over on an almost finished piece because it was cut too small can be a real pain. It is especially relevant for projects where you only have a small number of wood or complex-piece projects. Starting in these cases can be too time-consuming, if not impossible.

- So, begin right by double-checking your measurements habitually, and you can spare yourself a real headache later on.

2.8 A Marking Knife

- A marking knife is used, with your saws and chisels, to mark where you will be cutting. You need the right marking knife to get into tight spots (such as dovetails) and make exact lines (which is essential for tight-fitting joints). You'd think any old knife is going to work, but you'd be wrong.

- Label Your Cut Parts as You Cut Them

- When you do more complex tasks, you will get into cases where you create several cuts for various sections, only to discover that you have messed up the separate pieces and scraps from your cuts. You then have to re-measure everything to figure out what's what.

- To mark/label your pieces as you cut them is the right solution. If you are using a soft lead pencil, afterward, you can easily sand off the title if necessary. If you like puzzles, you can ignore this tip.

- Cut Pieces a Little Larger

- To account for sanding, cutting errors, and other potential problems, cutting project pieces slightly larger than the required size is generally good practice, especially for a beginner. Remember, removing more material is much easier than re-adding once it's been removed.

2.9 Jack Plane

A Jack Hand plane is a bench plane of middle size. Some planes are so commonly used that they usually sit on the workbench. When you are on an account, you can temporarily use a jack plane instead of other planes carrying out specialized functions:

Rough removal of stock (if you purchase a second blade/iron and form it in a curved "camber") To help joint board edges (if the board does not exceed 3x the length of your jack plane) For smoothing of surfaces

Eventually, you're going to want to buy a delicate smoothing plane and jointer plane. However, a Jack Plane will help you start working! A modern and sharp Jack Plane would be perfect for professionals and beginners who aren't up to rehab a hand plane.

2.10 Block Plane

You will ease the square edges with a router for tasks touched by people's hands — gates, tables, anything with a handle. But there's nothing like a low-angle block plane for children — and how to use it under adult supervision. Block planes, the irons of which split transparent wood curls at an angle of 21 degrees, explode with life lessons. Take off a little stock at a time; feel the tool through the work, and work best with sharp tools. Woodworkers often place planes on their side when they do not need them to shield the iron's edge.

2.11 Work Clothes

There is nothing more beautiful and appealing than a kid ready to roll on a project in his or her cotton, in the context of home improvement and working with children. This one comprises a 9-ounce, mid-weight, 100% cotton duck with double knees and elastic braces on the shoulder; the bibs come in as many sizes as kids.

2.12 Tool Pouch

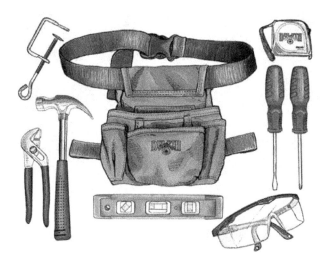

Also, in a tool pouch, there are life lessons:

Preparation.

Choose the best equipment for the task. Keep track of your stuff. The tool pocket for a kid is just plain fun, too. This tool pack comes with hand equipment and protective glasses. Screwdrivers, paper scales, pliers, and a wrench allow it even simpler to walk into the shop and produce it. A kid who carries his equipment, however, becomes a far more willing supporter.

2.13 Remodeling Hammer

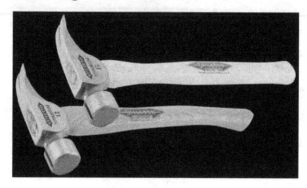

The 12-ounce remodeler hammer, shown above, is perfect for the child's woodwork. Yet at 12 ounces, the item is just as small as it gets and as easy to handle. Kids enjoy banging on things, so why not set up a board with a couple of nails in it and let them have it? And when they're done, you'll take back the excellent hammer so that they might not be able to destroy or outgrow and use it for their projects.

2.14 Hand Saw

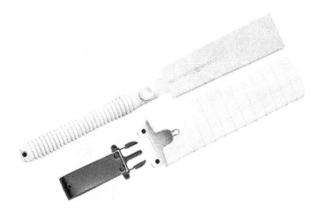

A perfect way to teach children to make stuff is by sawing boards — securely. Perhaps it is not the best course to give them a 15-pound worm drive, but a small, nimble Japanese-style pull-saw is. You can find hand saws that have replaceable blades that are super primo and not-so-pricey. They cut on the pull stroke, which is much simpler than any cutting on the push stroke. And they're sharp, with no threat. Plus, you will be able to use them when your kid doesn't need them. They are perfect for projects of all sorts.

2.15 Cordless Drill for Children

They are, sometimes, alluded to as Gimlets. They lack a hand brace's strength and the eggbeater hand drills' rpm, but they seem to function well, especially in greenwood.

Children have lots of toy drills. The thing is, they're just kids.

When your daughter or son has grown the invented tool, it might be time to find a practical device. A drill is a standard option, but then you can select an impact driver for your child.

There are the following considerations because children should have an impact driver:

- Suitable for smaller hands

- Low Voltage

- No large chuck with large openings and a rugged

textured ring

- No high strength required to tighten a chuck. They allow the use of a fast connector. Bits switch back and forth

- It's an instrument they will grow into, not a toy to be wasted.

Although it's tempting to buy one that fits the child's favorite color, you can get one that matches the tools you may have on the battery site/service. When you don't have a preference for the brand, then go for their favorite hue.

Such devices also come with no battery or are available with choices of the battery's size. Continuing with batteries like 1.5Ah - 2Ah is safer because they are both lightweight and lower in capacity. They are less costly too.

Buying a genuine impact driver can develop their abilities and ensure that they can be relocated for use to the mom or dad's workshop once they lose interest.

2.16 4-in-1 Device by Play Mat

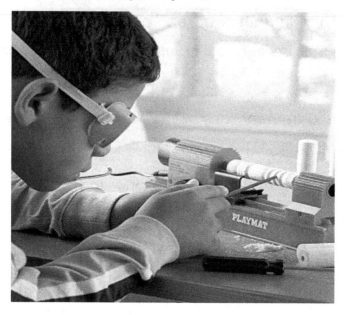

This **4-in-1 tool** available in the market is a blend of four electrical woodworking tools:

- Drill Press

- Disk Sander

- Lathe

- Jig Saw

Generally, it is convenient for a little machine. Your son will love molding the wood rod pieces on the lathe along with the thin plywood sheets provided in the package, being cut and sanded.

2.17 Children Tool Belts

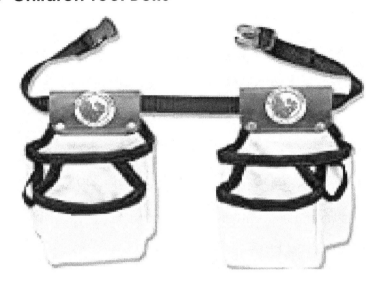

Part of the workshop time is related to learning skills, and part is a little dress-up. Children tend to imitate adults. They enjoy doing what parents do and wearing what parents wear. Your tool belt, however, partly mounted, would, of course, not suit the waist of your kid. It all comes off instantly. So much he needs to carry it that he ends up wearing it in both hands. After a few minutes, it becomes a security concern because he does not have any free hands to secure himself.

2.18 A bench hook for Kids

The objective of woodworking is to help young children to make things from the natural resource- wood. Thus, a friendly bench hook can help achieve this objective and assist children in doing three things.

It can help kids saw more precisely. There is no doubt that accurate cuts give a better shape and look to finished projects. Success fosters pride, and belief.

A bench hook for kids will assist them in sawing more effortlessly. It develops enjoyment and thrill in kids.

It is a safe tool, and when used correctly, it will not result in an accident and keep the hands of kids safe.

2.19 Toolbox Woodworking kits

Often kids don't initially have the patience to remain still when doing any of the pre-work to launch a little project. You don't have the patience to do the prep-task for your young woodworker to build a tiny project a few other days. And it is where any of the pre-manufactured kits could come in handy.

While the thought of a prefab kit may often annoy the woodworker, it is often quite convenient to have quick access to take a tool off the shelf and get to work on it instantly with the child. You can get a toolbox that has a whole line of workbench and tools. They should be kid-sized but genuine.

2.20 Workbench for a child

The parents need to invest in a suitable workbench. A good workbench is essential for a happy, safe, and secure experience with kids working in the workshop. A suitable workbench should have the following attributes:

- Configurable rack

- Storage

- Large work surface

- Dog holes

You must have noticed that it lacks the presence of a vise. The aim should be to teach children to preserve their work correctly to prevent both frustration and accidents.

2.21 Child-Sized Workmate

To keep small hands off the wood as they are screwing, drilling, sawing, chiseling, or nailing, you must make sure to keep the work-piece clamped. Injuries happen when children use their hands to hold the work-piece.

If you're selecting your child's actual workmate to use, pick the one with the step to put on. It does not just add a little height to your kids, and it also adds their weight to the bench so it cannot slip. It also has a 450 lb. capacity, just in case you require it for your own needs.

2.22 Saws for Kids

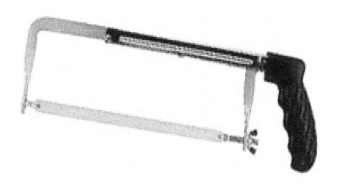

The protection will be the first condition before your child can use a handsaw. Safeguard the wood with helpful miter-box, clamps, or vises. Children will be instructed to place both hands on the saw or one side behind the back. It would remove nearly any possible accidents that could take place during the sawing process. With that, the next task is to select the saw that is just right for your kid. There are a few options, as with all woodworking tool selection decisions.

2.23 Hack Saws

Hack saws for cutting metal are indeed a great starter wooden saw for children. The teeth are not too hostile and are thin. It makes launching quick and going back or forth easy. The teeth are designed to hold up to a decent quantity of abuse and offer a relatively good cut. The blade isn't quite large, so it doesn't get as quickly lodged in the wood as a traditional wood saw. The saw blade may be turned over as an extra incentive, and it can be adjusted to either cut on the push or the pull stroke. Make sure to find one with tensions at both ends of the blade, not one of the thin ones where the blade end is not protected. Replacement blades are reasonably plentiful and affordable. When they are willing to use a genuine wooden saw, this can serve its real purpose of slicing wood and will be a means that might last throughout their lifetimes.

2.24 Pull Saws

Pull-saws come in a range of sizes and shapes, with teeth cutting on the pull-stroke. The false teeth are typically sharper than conventional saws, so the blades are smaller, which means cutting is more comfortable and faster with them. The carpenter type saws are recommended for use as they have only one side of teeth. The double-sided saws are useful, with one side designed for cutting rip and the other for crosscutting, but the existence of teeth on both surfaces of the blade poses a little more health danger for youngsters. The one downside to pull saws is that if misused, the teeth are too sharp and broke relatively quickly.

2.25 Toolbox Saws

The toolbox saws are thin and have a stronger blade that renders them exceptionally robust in general. The handle of plastic lets it appear like a doll, but it is not. Both the push and pull movement cut the wood, so it cuts quickly and effectively. The blade shield is safe and covers up the teeth entirely, and it keeps them away from children who violently pick up their devices and put them away. It is an excellent saw for children.

2.26 Coping Saws

Kids can better avoid handling saws or jigsaws. When used by little kids, the blades sometimes bind and crack. They take more time than the parents to know and learn how to handle these saws, and a more careful hand to let them work. Most parents do the error of beginning their children with a coping saw as they seem smaller and convenient for kids, but either of the saws shown above is a safer option.

2.27 Kid Tool Set Safety

While a set of tools comes with a variety of tools, nonetheless, the parents should be wise enough to introduce one tool at a time to their kids. They can introduce one tool after seven days or more. In this way, it would be much simpler to address function and teach kids about **tool safety**. Now let us go through the specific rules for handling saws safely and effectively:

- Children need to keep both hands on the saw.

- Children should only saw on wood in the vise. They can also saw on wood in the **miter box**.

- It is strongly recommended that no sawing should be done on furniture.

There are some tools in the set that need to be postponed for months or even years before you believe the device is ideal for the child's age, ability, and behavior.

2.28 Final Word on Saws

Whatever kind of saw you chose for your kid, kids, and

parents must realize that sawing is a good act. Many children get the wrong idea when they see their parents that sawing is an offensive, strong act; the more you push, the faster you strike. The harder you hang onto the saw, the more comfortable you cut. Both are wrong. A saw should be gently pushed and softly pulled to make the teeth do the job. A saw should be held gently, not stiffly. The basic concept is that if something is clenched (hands, teeth, butt) while you are sawing, You're doing something inappropriate with your sawing tool.

2.29 Step-stool Tool Box

The Stack-On Step N toolbox will help your son balance on it when operating on the workbench, and then put his equipment in it when it's over.

These are larger than the most average size toolbox and are well built to be safe for children or adults, especially when standing on them. It's estimated to carry as much as 325lbs. These stacks up just fine, should you buy more than one. In addition to its role as a step stool and toolbox, your son may even use it as a workbench and a bench.

Chapter 3: Types of Wood and How to Start off with Wood working

There are two types of solid wood- softwoods and hardwoods- to choose from.

Hard Wood

Hardwood is generally the wood from a deciduous tree that has left, including oak or maple. And they tend to be harder, physically, than softwoods. An interesting exception would be Balsa, an extremely softwood, but it is hardwood as the Balsa tree is deciduous. The term hardwood is used to describe the physical rigidity of the wood.

Soft Wood

Softwood is a wood that originates from a conifer tree, usually with cones and needles. It is similar to a pine tree.

The softness of wood can be checked using your nail.

Expansion & Shrinkage in Woods

All strong timber may be vulnerable to contraction and expansion. The boards will get moisture during rainy or humid months, causing them to swell. And they compress when they lose the moisture in drier months. Expansion and contraction are essential areas to consider while working with hardwood. It would be best if you kept this factor in mind. Be mindful of movement in wood on significant ventures.

3.1 Remember in choosing the best tools that kids are too immature for some tools

You require a set of furniture-safe play tools so children can play with them in spaces where actual tools wouldn't be suitable in the car, or the living room, or at the grandma's home. They require freedom to explore while they aren't monitored and instructed, no hammering with a screwdriver, no playing with the saw, no sticking the drill in your head, etc.

A Guide to Woodworking with young children

Woodwork is a perfect way to help kids work in their 'proximal growth environment.' Children can often do and learn is often expanded by open-nature woodworking, which needs children to be problem solvers. Kids also imitate what they see people doing, and through instruction, kids get great joy in learning different things and doing something they previously did not do.

Woodworking presents children with an outstanding play

scenario to participate in problem-solving-a vital experience for children to build towards their future at an early age. Children must also improve eye-hand coordination, spatial perception, sense of direction, and learn how to properly use potentially harmful tools.

What if you do not know much about woodworking?

If you have little experience using carpentry tools, why not take up the learning challenge alongside the kids. The most important thing when you just start is to take your time. Start with what you're happy with, and go there. Children can communicate more easily with you while you take your time, and that will boost their trust, and you will soon be shocked by what they (and you!) can achieve.

Woodworking is not gender-specific

Indeed, gender is meaningless. It can surely be achieved by women/girls too! If they are enabled and encouraged, they can be as professional and as involved. In this area, both boys and girls will learn skills, competence, and trust.

3.2 An excellent opportunity for children to learn from more skilled children

Older kids and kids more experienced in woodworking will

be watched and copied by those less familiar and unsure about what to do and how to do it. It's not unusual for kids to encourage one another or spot on a woodwork bench while someone is having trouble with what they want to do and subsequently standing up to provide support.

Setting up

Parents do not need to worry much when it comes to helping their kids with woodworking. They can start simple.

WORKBENCH

It is unnecessary to provide a devoted bench for carpentry at home, but a kid needs some table surface. It is because kids cannot see, and some of the things they want to do cannot be done on the ground.

A workbench is needed in early childhood centers to ensure that all tools and wood are kept together and made accessibly. Based on the task children perform, a 1200 mm x 600 mm workbench may be used comfortably for up to four children whether they are gluing and not sawing; for example, two children will be required to stand at the bench. For the children using it, the bench should be around the waist height. The bench should be around waist height for the children using it.

WOOD

The children must select and envision getting several different pieces of wood and a healthy supply. Workshops, some hardware stores, construction businesses, tree-cutters, and sawmills may be able to help and provide free off-cuts.

Do not use treated wood H4 or H5 as it contains arsenic salts, which are toxic when converted into sawdust.

When everything else fails, what you will consider are 4 cm to 10 cm high branches. Branches that are 4 cm to 10 cm thick can be perfect for sawing and easy to handle in contrast with pinewood quality furniture. House clearance companies have frequently destroyed tables that they are happy to throw away because they have little interest. Pallets are often secure and can be easily removed with a pry bar and a hammer.

Large logs about 40 cm wide and between 25 cm -30 cm high create excellent single workbenches for children.

When they work, they will put nails up on the top. Driftwood, while somewhat smoother than usual wood, is perfect for learning how to saw.

VISES AND CLAMPS

Children don't have the power to grip a piece of wood and

break it like an adult with one hand, so the first move is to show them how to use a muzzle or G-clamp to keep the wood still.

Some kids might need some help to get the necessary clamping force to stop the wood movement. Have them tighten the vice as much as they can, and then give them the final turn. Move on to the next stage, once the wood is securely in place.

Vises should be bought from hardware shops and locked to the bench to keep them from shifting. The engineer's vises are preferable as they are much easier to attach to the workbench and prevent children from sawing into the top of the bench. Or if there's ample overhang on the benchtop, a decent alternative is a pair of G-clamp vises. They are inexpensive and can be moved easily-two can be placed into line for large pieces of wood.

SAWS

It's quite challenging to use a saw when all you know is that you need to push it back and forth as fast and as hard as possible. That is a dangerous approach. When kids manage to start the cut-off and get through the wood, they will see the final cut through the wood, eliminating any resistance, and the saw will start moving across the table driven by the boy's weight. A backstop in the form of a plywood sheet behind the saw is perfect, as it can harmlessly stop the saw when a child slips.

Having the child draw a pencil line or mark on top of the wood is the best method to get the cut started. Place the saw at the mark, close to the handle, then draw the saw backward with a little force. Then, again put the saw on and draw it back. Having created a groove of about 5 mm, get the child to push the saw slightly forward and backward until the groove is about 2 cm deep. And that's the aspect of lightness and delicacy.

They can apply themselves honestly now. Remember that a three or four-year-old will require all the strength and body weight to get the saw to work and have no strength left to correct when finally cut through. You can be prepared if you know what will happen next. When the saws lose teeth, buy cheap saws, and replace them – which they will do over time.

PLIERS

Pliers are typically used to pick stuff up and to take items out. Pliers look very similar to scissors once the child gets

accustomed to picking items up, using them like tongs.

Avoid using pliers with cutters because if a finger is stuck, this may be harmful. Small electronic pliers are the right size for kids and are accessible readily. Generally, they are about half the height of the engineering pliers.

NAILS AND HAMMERS

Adults may fear that kids can hit each other if they let kids have hammers. But there's always a chance that kids could strike each other with specific items like blocks from the block corner or sandpit spades. It is a case of supervision, observing children, and making sure hammers (and other tools) are used for the intended purposes.

Talk to kids about lifting the hammer no higher than their head height for safety reasons-this prevents them from accidentally hitting themselves or another child behind them. Kid-size hammers or small hammers can be bought from hardware stores. Shortening a regular wooden-handled hammer length is an inexpensive and simple exercise, requiring a regular saw only.

Display and demonstrate the wrist's usage to youngsters, then swing the hammer to strike the nail. When the child has developed trust in using the shorter hammer, they will continue gripping the nail and get going themselves.

When kids master starting a nail off inside a piece of wood, they can get a full-size hammer and achieve better results with a little more instruction. If necessary, a cloth peg around the nail's bottom side can be useful in saving small fingers from being hurt.

The urge to choose cheap panel pins must be resisted when selecting nails, as this bend over quickly. Long nails move into the wood and inflict harm to the bench or floor underneath. Plaster clouts are inexpensive, and length is just fine. Seek other sizes too, when the kids become confident with clouts. You must avoid the use of large nails as they are designed to be put in with a heavier hammer that a child cannot handle.

SCREWDRIVERS AND SCREWS

For little hands, a little fat crosshead screwdriver and screws fit great. An electronic screwdriver may be an excellent tool, but they typically require a lot of time to charge, like electronic drills.

DRILLS

Usually, cordless drills are used to drill holes and push screws in. Some of the cheaper 12-volt ones don't have much capacity. Many preschoolers may use a fair 12volt cordless drill competently, but it's necessary to supervise again. The parent will remain within the child's range to ensure the kid's welfare if required. At the bottom of the handle, cordless drills have a ton of weight, which counteracts the torque, and typically have a clutch mechanism that gives some power over the force used. They do have keyless chucks with fewer places for tangling stuff like hair in – but long hair (on boys and girls, and adults) should still be pulled back into a ponytail while using some equipment, especially drills.

Another type of drill is a hand drill. There are two commonly available varieties-a plastic one with a winding handle that looks like a standard electric drill and a geared one made of metal. Of the two, the metal is a sturdier model, but it's quite big, so it can be challenging for smaller kids (although most 4 to 5-year-olds won't have a problem). The one made of plastic is perfect, although it will not last as long. The metal drill can accommodate more significant drill pieces.

A vice or clamp should hold the wood for protection while operating the hammer, as it requires two hands to work a hammer, whether mechanical or electronic. The maximum that most children can try to pierce a 10 mm thick pine slice is about 10 mm. A 7 mm to 8 mm bit is usually adequate. Educational suppliers typically market drill bits from 3.5 mm to 4 mm, but the larger drill bit has the benefit of avoiding the sideways pressure children exert on them. Often the wire nails are used as inexpensive drill bits, but they don't work very well.

Children may attempt to strike the nails with the drill, so parents should get the drill sharpened once a month. When you make use of plastic drills, you need to check them regularly. Metal drills usually come with the promise of a lifetime. It is recommended to have a cheap cordless drill, but this is not essential.

Other accessories

In addition to the tools as mentioned above, make sure that kids have the following:

Sandpaper

To ensure a suitable size for children, parents need to cut the sandpaper into half or quarters. Moreover, parents should supply smooth, rough, and coarse sandpaper to kids.

Ruler

All you require is a folding ruler or a long rigid ruler. It is useful to draw lines on flat wood for older children. It also helps to introduce older children to numbers that can be used to help them learn about measuring.

Carpenter's pencil

Children may draw a dot or a cross to mark where they'll hammer in a nail. Pencil markings may also be used to indicate when to begin sawing.

PVA glue

It is an essential element since it helps kids learn how to join and fix things.

Paper

Paper is usually used for framed pictures, sails, and decorations.

Water-based paint and brushes

These will help instill creative skills in children.

Plastic milk bottle tops

These make lights and great wheels. Besides, a string for guitar strings, pull-strings to attach to the children's toys, etc., and anything else for decorations or other purposes such as foil, cloth scraps, fake fur, even leaves, could help children to improve and develop their natural abilities.

Socket set

Invest in a children's socket kit, and build items with nuts and bolts. Children will more conveniently use the socket set to secure the bolts than spanners.

3.3 Starting Off

One way to start is by using one type of tool for a few days or weeks (depending on the frequency of use). It makes the kids use each resource better and more straightforward because you can also demonstrate many kids together. Wait before the kids become aware of the tools and correctly use the tools before adding more tools.

It is beneficial to think about what needs to be done ahead of time, especially if you decide to quit the woodworking area. The area is always in need of close oversight.

3.4 Communicate Safe behavior and rules to kids

Kids must be taught and ensured to comply with the following rules:

• Tools should not be above the kids' height.

• Kids should not run around carrying tools.

• The tools must never be removed from the workbench area.

• Kids must learn to use each tool correctly. The children will need to be given a demonstration on the proper use and handling of tools.

• Children must use safety earmuffs to protect hearing.

• Children should always be wearing shoes when working with tools.

3.5 Extending the learning and the fun

It's time to let the creativity run and keep the fun going, especially once kids get involved and get accustomed to using tools. Below are only a handful of practical ideas:

Framed photos-Create photo frames for a drawing or a painting. Use cardboard for the back. Attach a string to the back for hanging the frame onto the wall.

Airplanes: You can start with three small lengths of wood. First, cut the wood to size for the plane's main body, the back wing, and the front wing. Then you can add a propeller. It can be done by drilling a hold in the center for the nail. It will allow the propeller to turn quickly.

Guitars:

1. Use a flat piece of wood, and nail a long stick to it.

2. Attach string lengths to the nails at each end.

3. Paint it with your favorite color.

Signs – You can make street signs, garden signs, or name signs by first nailing a stick to a wooden board. Next, you can use a pencil to write phrases like Stop, Go, Vine, Molly's House. Finally, you can give it your favorite color.

Push cart-The construction of a push kart is a perfect idea whether you or another person has any experience in carpentry or not. The 100 mm x 40 mm decking creates a perfect foundation. Wheels can be acquired from old bikes. Additionally, an old plastic patio chair can function as a seat. You need to help children create this fabulous pushcart. To help the kids whenever they get stuck. Children will have a lot of fun. Plus, they will learn some excellent skills in creating this pushcart.

3.6 How the Parents of a kid helped their child in learning the woodworking

My child always loved to help. He loves tools, and he has a set of pretend play tools. However, at the same time, he's the perfect age to start some real woodworking of his own, so we got him woodworking set for his fifth birthday.

We looked at many commercial tools for kids, but none of them had all the stuff we needed, all of them had items we didn't want or need, and several of them were very costly, so we opted to put together our kit of the woodwork.

3.7 Woodworking Set

We included the following tools in our woodworking set for Noah:

A kid-sized hammer – lightweight hammers are inexpensive and straightforward to locate in most hardware shops; make sure you have one with a claw so that you can use it to extract and hammer the nails!

Nails – they must be rather long and should have a large head for beginners.

Drill bits along with a hand drill.

A clamp or vice: It helps to keep things intact while securing them. Moreover, it makes it simpler and better to firmly clamp stuff in place.

A ruler and pencil for measuring and labeling – a tape measure are excellent too, but more challenging for little hands to accurately measure.

Wood glue: It provides an easy way to fix small objects and decorations.

Sandpaper: We bought sandpaper of different weights.

We also purchased water-colored paints and markers for the project's decoration.

Various broken pieces that can be nailed, attached, or hammered-plastic bottle caps are simple to drill and then nail on, foam shapes glue quickly, beads stick and nail quickly.

Wood – you'll need to select softwood from a variety of

woods. Many hardware stores can offer you free pine sticks, and you may also inquire at construction sites (make sure the pine isn't treated) or check for programs that include recycled art and craft supplies. You can also slice up small logs and sticks if you have firewood, and a large old lump of wood or a stump is a great and safe surface to hammer on or drill on.

We have ambitions to introduce a handsaw, but not until Noah becomes more familiar with the basics and can handle such an advanced tool in the fundamentals and willing to do so. We are also looking at a hack saw, especially the one which is small, easy to use, and capable of cutting various stuff.

3.8 Woodworking with Kids

When they first began using the tools, they wanted a little guidance and encouragement, so it's crucial to teach the kids how to use the tools safely. It is an activity that, at first, required a lot of oversight. Still, as they became more confident and capable, less oversight is needed – just a quick reminder about safety and being on hand to help out when it is direly required.

We gave Noah a large chunk of firewood. Then we taught (five) him hammering nails into that piece of wood. A broad, solid surface indicated that he was just concerned about the nail and the handle, not about what he was hammering against.

To get the feel of hammering, it took a couple of practice and a few bashed fingers, but eventually, Noah was pounding in the nails without too much difficulty. The parents should not hesitate to teach the children how to use the hammer's claw to pick nails.

It requires a bit of power and skill, but the digging of holes in objects is just something advantageous! The children are always gathering various recyclables and saying, 'may I poke a hole in that? 'For beginners, soft plastics such as lids and containers are perfect.

It is not often possible to bind pieces of wood together with screws, but it is simple to stick tiny parts and irregular shapes by applying some woodworking glue or a low temp hot glue gun. Woodworking is ideal for the learning and development of kids. It provides numerous chances for problem-solving, situational perception, and the application of a range of abilities. Besides, woodworking is a fantastic creative medium for the kids. Building something with just nails and wood can be a little tricky.

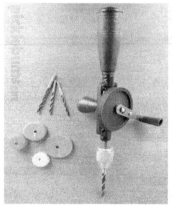

Moreover, to make it the way you want is a bit more challenging. However, adding loose parts and markers or paints makes adding those little touches easy to make your first project as you want it to. All our kids loved hammering and grinding and building using a platform they don't get to explore enough. It has been great fun to get into woodworking.

Chapter 4: Easy Woodworking Projects for Kids

It gives you so much satisfaction to create something with your own hands. If you have a handy kid, let him amaze you with what he can while he is involved in woodworking projects. You only have to instruct your child to use tools correctly, and the things he will do with them are remarkable. We have put together some of the most common simple craft projects that are child-friendly and budget-friendly. Many of these projects need materials that are usually available in the house. Woodcrafts are one of the most beautiful activities to do with the tiny ones since they are such an excellent teaching activity and still encourage kids to discover nature! To locate different forms of wooden items such as twigs, trees, or discarded wooden fragments, take them out for a stroll and show them along the way what the various wood uses are that is, creating paper we write and draw on, constructing homes and houses we reside in, preparing sports equipment such as baseball bats and also furniture.

With those wood crafts for kids, you can encourage your child. It will inspire your kid to go out and appreciate the real world. This list begins with the most straightforward projects requiring a few extra materials and few to no devices.

4.1 Twig ABC's

This scheme is the simplest in the whole list. Preschool Toolkit is meant for preschool kids learning the alphabet and has a record of precisely the twigs you and your kid make all letters from A - Z. Make a walk stroll into a learning opportunity in the park! You can cut the twigs easily to the size you need if you have to. Does your kid know the ABC's already? Start practicing with easy three-letter words, and help your child reading and writing these letters.

4.2 Colorful Wind Mobiles

Here are another fun and the quick wood project you can experience with children of any age and extra microscopic materials. Not only can this project build a lovely smartphone to hang outdoors, but it also teaches the kid a fundamental technical principle such as compression and tension. It is an excellent way to use yarn scraps as a treat that you can have around. When your kid grows up with this simple art to be a famous engineer, they will thank you for encouraging them!

4.3 Tie All of It Together

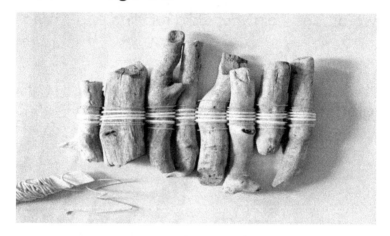

With this excellent but straightforward art project that is ideal for all ages, a day at the beach can last forever. No local beach? Go to your backyard for a short walk or to collect sticks of different lengths. You will never let your child leave behind all that driftwood back on the soil, and they're going to get a reminder of an enjoyable beach day.

4.4 Use leftover pieces to make creative artworks.

Do the remaining pieces of wood from various art ventures overflow your house? Here's a good idea to use them all up in an easy way! Your kid will have fun drawing and painting, and you'll love to see their imagination taking a trip with the endless forms they will bring together with pieces of wood.

4.5 Nature Royalty

What kind of child doesn't like wearing a crown? If your family enjoys Julia Donaldson's book "Stick Guy," then your children have almost definitely amassed enough sticks to create a comfortable and cute stick crown inspired by the leading character. Simple enough to help preschool kids and kindergarteners, it's an exciting way for kids to create something new and can wear to show off!

4.6 A Lovely Wooden Frame

Young kids like to make presents for their loved ones. Whether for Valentine's Day, Mother's Day, or just because, it's not easy to ignore this quick to build a picture. With some of the craft store's cheap, prefabricated wooden frames and some paint or a cookie cutter (heart-shaped), your children can have much too much enjoyable dipping their thumbs in the paint for this craft! It's shockingly easy, complicated, and completely worth it for an eternal reminder of when the thumbs of your kids were that tiny!

4.7 A lovely Photo Frame

Try out this stunning frame influenced by nature when dreaming about picture frames as presents, especially if you can't take another macaroni bracelet or Play-Dough cup. You have everything you need to build this beautiful and sentimental picture frame with some cheap items from the nearest craft shop and a trip outside with the preschooler. Add a photo of your child using it to frame some of their favorite artists for your lounge.

4.8 It is time to sail

When you have a or a glue gun, no matter how many sticks your kid can find, you can build an armada of sailboats! With a small application of your creative abilities, you and your kid may spend a little time playing shipbuilders as you wish. Place them on a blue paper and take a sailing ride or go for an expedition worldwide!

4.9 A Keepsake that can last Forever

You might have a friend who loves to cut woods, or you may do it by yourself. Maybe you only enjoy purchasing pre-made crafts materials. However, you can have them, collect some slices of wood and paint, then get set to make some priceless keepsakes with your kids. The most acceptable part of this plan is that you can finish it in any color you want, and you can do as many handprints as you like, or you can go for only one per piece!

4.10 Sliced Wood Ornaments for Christmas

While gathering pieces of wood, be sure to keep some to beautify your Christmas tree for some of these festive crafts. It is an economical way to make decorations to keep or to offer as gifts. It would be best if you allowed the imagination to run wild and draw on as many imaginative ideas about how and when to create, like images of monograms, Santa, and snowmen. As your kids grow up, you'll love to find them in your bin's holiday decorations. It will also remind you of the time when you created these with your kids when they were pretty young!

4.11 Create an eye-catching Web and Spider

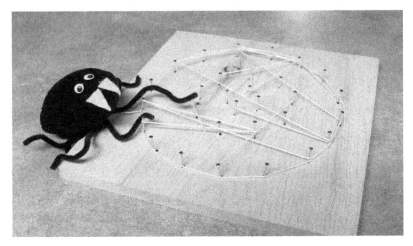

It is not finished yet! Here's another thing you can do with a hammer, some screws, and some string or rubber strips. Create a pattern on a square wood slab and, if you are sure they're prepared, let your kids go along the pattern to hammer the nails. Kids then build a spider's web using the rubber string or bands – and then cut it apart to construct fresh webs repeatedly.

4.12 An easy to Make Catapult

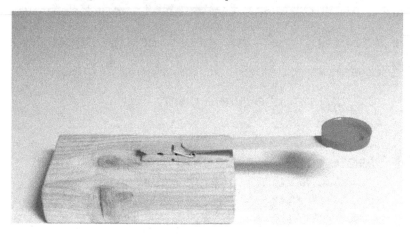

Half the materials required to build this catapult ideal for small children are a fundamental piece of wood and a wooden clothespin. You should let your child use cotton balls as missiles; that is a perfect idea to save your fixtures from the projectiles! Children will use pointers or brush to design their catapults, whereas you have to monitor and control the hot glue yourself. The only problem now is: How to clean all the cotton balls?

4.13 Create a Big Catapult

When your children have grown past clothespin crafts, get them for some 2x4s to the hardware shop and saws. You can help them to build a much heavier version of a catapult. Older rank school kids can evaluate, carve, hammer, and screw a pair of wood blocks and planks together under parents' supervision. Select small items to help them make this Catapult. Once they're done, you have to make sure that they don't target the neighbors and friends' yards. This one is an artwork meant for the outside!

4.14 Topsy Turvy

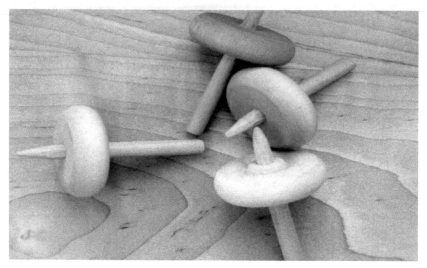

For these old-fashioned toys, adults certainly have to prepare, but kids can always have lots of fun drawing and working! You'll need to determine how much to allow your kid to do. A minimal amount of effort here provides a lot of playtimes. No matter how digitalized the home may be or how hooked the kids are to computers, spinning tops are an everlasting cause of fun!

4.15 Say Cheese!

It's only a matter of time before children understand how everyone needs to capture their images. With this imaginative wooden device, you can create something your talented kid will switch right back to you! No prominent instruments are needed, but preschoolers can assist with gluing and painting together with the pieces. All you need can be conveniently found across the house or at art shops. It is a toy that you would not mind your child playing with for a long time!

4.16 Homemade Stamps

When your kid discovers logs that are very large for the log creations, it's time to bring some sandpaper, a saw, and a few little items out there. It is a beautiful art, and you can help your child make several wooden stamps. Hold some paint on hand on rainy days, and you will always have an innovative project ready to help your child make some craft in the spare time!

4.17 Little Robot

These wooden DIY robots are the most excellent thing ever! It is simpler than it would appear. Create a treat for a kid or pre schooler yourself, or support high school and older kids with necessary equipment and woodblocks. You'll make sufficient for a whole robot army to take over the creativity of your child before you know it!

The building is one of the most straightforward tasks for kids. Each one is intended to please the younger ones. It's going to be like having a robot pal for your family, one that's large enough to keep the kids happy and is made up of small enough pieces so that kids get the feel of playing with blocks.

A wooden buddy robot is simple enough to build. You can

use your creativity and imagination to create this wooden robot buddy. It's also a concept that makes it possible for the child's imagination to run wild during the creation process.

4.18 Wooden DIY Bird Feeder

This garden bird feeder needs adult supervision. Select twigs that are heavier, thicker, and more durable than the small sticks from other design ventures and use real peanut butter for the glue. This project is perfect for younger and older children alike, and parents should help them create this stunning bird feeder. The older kids should do the hammering, while the little children should put up the birdseed and peanut butter. So, pick up those binoculars and see all the fun buddies coming in for a snack from your backyard window!

4.19 Little library

Not only can small libraries offer a means for children to learn how to create

items, use their visualization, and obey directions, but they also understand the importance of interacting with others. You can even enroll it once you've finished so that people can stop and see what your kids have created outside your home.

As you build, you'll want to have in mind the environment, so if you stay anywhere where it rains too much, you'll want to consider a covered roof to keep dry everything you want

to share.

4.20 Kids' workbench

A workbench is a perfect place to show kids that they often have to create stuff they'd use for daily use. If you're a smart dad, that is precisely the sort of stuff that you'll like your kids to pick up. Besides, it will provide them a chance to think that they are grown-up a little more when they start collecting their toolset.

Like other stuff, this is potentially something you would create using your creative and imaginative skills.

4.21 The bee house

This one is good for children who enjoy nature too. Creating a pollinator house provides a habitat for bees, making the children know they are improving the environment. The best thing is that these types of bees occasionally bite, and it's a reasonably healthy opportunity for your children to support bees who will keep your garden blooming.

This job isn't that complex. Moreover, the most challenging device to use in this project is just a drill. You'll either want to do it yourself or offer a lot of advice to your kids. You'll always want to bear that this comes with a canopy to protect the bees from flooding, and you have to design it so that it is as safe from water as possible.

4.22 Wooden planter

It is the other straightforward project, so if your children are in seeds, it's a perfect start to a summer-long plan to make a relatively small yard. They can begin with some necessary plank fastening and wind up with peppers or radishes or some basil.

Much like every other child project, this one can be personalized based on your designs or what you will like your completed plant to look like.

4.23 Birdhouses

Without birdhouses, no collection of woodworking DIY projects will be sufficient for children. These are good intermediate projects which every child makes up at some point in their childhood. They provide your well-feathered friends with living space and encourage your children to take more complex actions in dealing with wood and equipment.

4.24 The Folding camp chair

If you're an outdoor person, a folding chair is a simple, easy collapsible project that will provide you with a place to rest while you're in the Fantastic Outdoors. If used by a bonfire playing the guitar or by a river tying a harness to a casting line, the children can love dreaming about their possible adventures while studying how to deal with wood as well as tying leather to furniture.

It is not only an easy project to build; it's also very inexpensive to put together.

4.25 Kids are playing and camping tent.

There's not a lot of woodworking here, practically. It's only fastening some wooden poles together and attaching sheets of fabric along a beam that holds them together.

However, the kids will still care if This ensures that, in less than 10 minutes, they can create a fort in the backyard. Would you still want them to learn to do this and give your kids hours of fun economically? You have to give your child a template so he can stoke his imagination.

4.26 Balance board

For the daredevils inside your family, it's a simple and inexpensive idea. It's a smart way to keep the balance perfect by not running the chance of a chipped tooth or fractured collarbone. Plus, it'll be fun for your family to create this craft. It needs the usage of power devices, which may be a bit of joy for children who get frustrated by the comfort and ease of doing things.

Although it seems essential enough to be a mere creativity activity, you would always want to have the correct wheel proportions, so it does not get unbalanced.

4.27 Make a Stick Barn

Your child will find it easy to make an iconic Midwestern

barn with painted craft sticks. Moreover, it will look amazing when hanged on the kitchen fridge.

Paint nine red sticks for craft, six white sticks for craft, and four white sticks for the mini craft. Leave them to dry. Let your kid make green grass and a blue sky with a colored sheet of paper or colored pens on a rectangular piece of cardstock. Support her and then build the barn base by pasting vertically in the following design on the 11th row of art sticks: 2 red, one white, five red, one white, two red. Horizontally join the white sticks over the bottom and top and connect two in the center. Glue the mini craft to build the barn roof, sticking to the red cardstock. Fix the roof of the barn above the barn to the background. Cut a black

paper rectangle and fasten it to the barn. For the look of hay, take the paper bag's strips and crumple; stick to a black rectangle.

4.28 Practice to create a Jumbo Wooden Dice

Challenge your kids to play with these large, multicolored dice — or see them having a ball in their favorite games using the dice.

Let the kids add a different color on each side of wooden

blocks. Choose several shades of paper and draw circles out as the dice marks. Let the children count two sets of dots on all the blocks to glue in.

Chapter 5: Innovative Woodworking Projects for Kids

There are not many tasks and activities that can give you enjoyment, entertainment, and satisfaction as a woodworking project. You will love the feel of completing your first wood project with your budding kid. Children derive pleasure when they are allowed to put their creativity into practice in an exciting and straightforward woodworking project. They get a chance to use devices such as adults. Moreover, parents get the joy of spending time doing something worthwhile with the children, which encourages and generates the spirit that the family can enjoy for a long time.

We have compiled several projects that are perfect for children. They bring an array of challenges for the kids. It should build a series of tasks so you can switch from one to the next with increasing difficulty, especially if the children like to work with their hands. Some of them are very basic and only include wood, paint, and glue. Others demand power tools. That means they need a degree of adult supervision, too. The best thing is that kids will concentrate their imagination at their simplest. Moreover, the kids can focus their creative skills on the grounds so that there are no

incorrect responses.

In terms of supplies and fasteners, each has its own different needs. These also include guidance on using the raw materials and images and what the finished product will look like. Please select the right one for your children and make them enjoy every bit of fun. Your kid can do these easy woodworking projects in 1 to 2 hours. These easy and enjoyable projects need only a few tools.

5.1 Wind Spinners

These are especially great to watch and create. Irrespective of where the wind is coming from, south, the north, east, or west, they turn in a magnificent and

spiraling motion.

5.2 Tic-Tac-Toe game

It is effortless to make your own Tic-Tac-Toe game at home. A DIY wooden Tic-Tac-Toe game is excellent for people of all ages, especially for kids. Moreover, it makes an excellent handmade present.

It is pretty simple to teach your child to make his jigsaw puzzle at home.

5.3 Jigsaw Puzzle

It is pretty simple to teach your child make his own jigsaw puzzle at home.

5.4 Word-Art Signs

If you have little wood at your home along with some essential tools, then you can easily teach and guide your child to make his **word signs** in less than an hour.

5.5 Succulent Planter

You will need wood and a few tools to help your child make his planter in a concise period.

5.6 Candleholders

You can help and guide your child to transform a scrap tree branch or log into a beautiful candle holder. It will add to the optics and ambiance of your living room.

5.7 Carve wooden spoons

The style and design possibilities of kitchen utensils and spoons are infinite. It will allow your child to be exceedingly more creative, and at the same time, shall help to unleash his true innovative potential.

5.8 State outlines

These outlines and stencils make a great jigsaw, scroll saw, and band saw projects.

5.9 Welcome letter to the front door

It is effortless to help and guide your child to make a welcome letter for your house's front door.

5.10 Make wooden scoops

It can be a fun project for kids who enjoy woodturning. They will find it both entertaining and fascinating. Moreover, they will get the chance to use their creative skills in the process.

5.16 Make "HOME."

Your child can easily make alphabets constituting the word Home.

5.17 Pen or pencil holder

Making a pencil or pen holder is a lot of fun and a simple project for the kids.

5.18 Hexagon (Honeycomb) Wall Shelves

The floating hexagon shelves are easy to build. They also make a fun DIY woodworking project for your kid.

5.19 Trendy Candleholders

Though a bit challenging, but you can help your kid create these oval-shaped candle holders. They create a warm and relaxing environment.

5.20 Wood Bench

Teach your child to flawlessly assemble this **wooden bench**. Moreover, you will also need glue along with few screws to help your child complete this fabulous project in less than two days.

5.21 Storage bins

They make an easy beginner woodworking project for kids. You can use place bins in the kitchen or any other space.

5.22 Tree stump side tables

Help your child select a tree stump. Let the tree stump dry. Finally, then cut off the bark. Your child can process and complete it to make a beautiful and useful side table or nightstand.

5.23 Homemade candy dispenser

Did we mention it can be satisfying to have a woodwork

project? Building your candy dispenser is not only a good learning experience, but it's something that your kids will love to build because it will give them treats whenever they want.

It includes specific simple hand tools, and parents may have a little more research to do depending on age and knowledge of the motor skills.

Supplies to Build a Candy Dispenser

Given below are the different wooden parts and other materials that you would

require to build this candy dispenser:

2" x 6" board, 24 inches long

2 11/2" x 51/2" x 51/2" boards for base and top

1" x 1 7/8" x 11" board for the slide

2 11/2" x 13/4" x 51/2" boards for the sides

Pencil

Tape

Pocketknife

Wood glue

Sandpaper

1 peg or dowel which should be about ¼ inch in diameter and 4 inches long

1 dowel or peg about which should be about ¼ inch in diameter and 2 inches long

A pint or quart canning jar with a metal ring

A crosscut saw that would be used to saw across the grain

A ripsaw would be required to saw with the grain

Drill little which would be utilized for pre-drilling 2 ½ inch holes

Countersink bit

7/8" spade bit

12 wooden screws, each 2 ½ inches long

4 flat-head brads

Screwdriver

A small drill bit that would be used to pre-drill brad holes is jarring

Gumballs

Jellybeans

5.24 Building a Candy Dispenser

Step-by-step instructions for building a candy dispenser are given below:

1. Cut the boards as per specifications and smooth them with sand.

2. Then screw and glue the base onto the sides.

3. Draw an X with the pencil from corner to corner on the upper board.

4. Drill a 7/8" hole in the top board's center.

5. Screw and glue the top board on the base and sides. Next, sand the slide till it slides easily through the middle of the dispenser in the square opening.

6. Bore a hole of ¾ inch from the front of the slide. For the 4" dowel or peg, this would be used. Drill out a 1/2-inch cut from the rear of the slide. For the 2-inch dowel or peg, this would be used. Glue the 4-inch dowel or peg onto the slide in the front hole.

7. Move the slide into position until at the 4-inch peg, it stops. Draw a loop on the slide from the 7/8" opening on the top board.

8. Pierce a 7/8" hole 3/8" into the slide.

9. With the pocketknife and smooth sand, bevel the 7/8-inch slide hole.

10. Nail and Drill the top board to the container ring.

11. Push the slide into its place.

12. Fill Up the jar with candies as your dispenser is now complete.

5.25 Catapult

If you always dreamed of building a catapult, then making this homemade catapult is very easy. Moreover, it is a fun activity for kids of all ages!

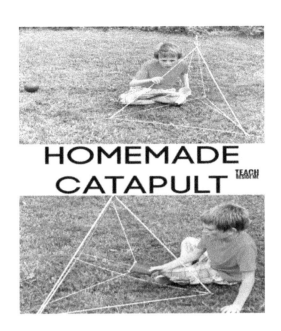

HOMEMADE CATAPULT

Catapult Learning Connections

Listed below are some of the facts concerning catapult:

Engineering

You will learn how to build a catapult that will last long.

Science

It is fantastic for a physics lecture. The process of pulling back and releasing can teach you about kinetic energy (energy of motion) and potential energy (stored energy). When you pull the cup back, you create potential energy. When you expel the energy and start a projectile, it is kinetic energy now.

Teach force and velocity. You can change the weight and size of the ball you use to catapult and test to see if it's going at a different height or distance.

History

You should be astonished to know that catapults have been around for several years!

How to Build a Catapult?

It is an easy project! Most of the kids could easily make this. Moreover, you do not need to glue guns for this one!

Supplies to Build a Catapult

Given below are the different wooden parts and other materials that you would require to build this catapult:

Six wooden dowels - 3 ft long. These are also readily available at the craft store.

Nine large rubber bands

Small plastic cup

Single-hole punch

Scissors

Small balls or any other balls of your choice to launch

Let's begin with building the structure of the catapult. First, make use of three of the wooden dowels. Create them in a triangular shape by sticking the corners with latex bands.

Then you pick up another three dowels and attach them as a triangle. However, it must look like a pyramid. You can add one at a time. You should start from each corner of the first triangle. You then connect them using a rubber band.

Now, take the plastic cup and punch three equidistant holes in it.

Break-in half three rubber bands, then attach them into the cup's gaps. The other ends of the rubber bands need to be tied to the top of the catapult and two corners at the bottom. To make this work, you'll need some larger rubber bands. If the rubber bands are not big enough, tie on to the ends of three more runner bands so they can extend the dowels down.

Place a ball in the cup, take it back and let it go! Now you've finished constructing a catapult. Everybody'll be impressed. And you need not tell them how easy it was!

5.26 DIY String Art on Wood

This art gives you the liberty to make custom pieces that match your color scheme, style, and personality. This simple DIY project can be completed in less than one hour, and most of the supplies of the string art are stuff you have on hand or you can take from the hardware shop.

This one can work for every shape and any string color scheme. You can select classic white or something funnier: it's up to you!

It will take at the most about 3 hours, and you and your child will be able to create this in shifts too.

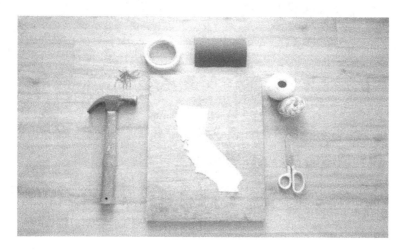

Supplies to Build String Art

Given below are the different wooden parts and other materials that you would require to build this string art:

- Wood

- Nails

- String

- Hammer

- Scissors

- Sandpaper

- Template

- Masking tape

The wood scale always depends on choice, although it is advised that you take a print of the ideal size of the pattern before heading to the woodshop to select it because you can see the undesirable space around the string. It creates hideous traces and attracts dust, making sure that masking tape does not leave glue on the surface.

Building a String Art

Step-by-step instructions for building a string art are given below:

First, smooth it with sandpaper.

Take out the Model and print. Stay careful around the corners! Do not hammer immediately by cutting on the pattern, as there will be bits and pieces of paper sticking on the nails that will take more time picking it out than merely scratching out the template.

Step back after you have fixed the map to make sure it's accurate. Masking tape helps hold the diagram in position but reduces the risk of removing stain or paint off the wood. Make sure you put the nails close together. If you are having difficulty, you can use tweezers to keep the nails in place. When hammering the nails down, the most important thing to remember is that the nails should be very close to each other, allowing only enough room for the string to drift down the middle. Remember to be careful about the spikes' accurate hammering, going down the wood and along straight lines. The more closely spaced the nails, the neater and cooler the string art would be. You may opt to minimize individual sections of the diagram that have so many curves.

Place the artwork for a personal touch in your home town place! Attempt to the position that in an environment that will create as many long straight lines as possible.

Use any string color you want, or even combine string colors get imaginative with it!

Loop around the outer nail, carry it to the heart's nails, loop it, and bring it to the next state nail. Just loop once per state nail before continuing onto the next. Nevertheless, tend to use the same core nail for the successive loops. It makes for great tension between the nails. To one core tooth, there will be almost fifteen state nails. It necessarily varies on the preference of the crafter. Don't be afraid to cut the string and start again until the right ratio is achieved.

Tie the string tail-end to the keys so that it gets fixed properly. It will not be the last of the string art ideas you're using to create fun artwork.

5.27 Serving tray

Your child can easily create a stylish and straightforward tray. He will find it handy to offer breakfast beautifully.

5.28 Bookends

These bookends are trendy yet very easy to make. Your child will enjoy creating these bookends.

5.29 Bathroom wall shelf

The wall-mounted shelf, which is simple to build, fits a lot into a limited space. A towel bar along with two shelves make this shelf a perfect storage unit for the bathroom.

5.30 Traditional Toolbox

It gives a perfect way to carry small instruments. In general, it has an offset handle that makes it easy to manage.

5.31 Glass bottle and wood vase

If you have some soda bottles, a 1 x 6 board, and are willing to spend about one hour with your kind, you can easily create this beautiful container for a splendid display of cut flowers.

5.32 Knife block

Teach your child to learn how to make your knife block. This knife block can easily hold kitchen knives of various sizes.

5.33 Simple Step Stool

You can help your child create a simple step stool. It is a simple woodworking project that requires little effort to make a splendid piece.

5.34 Portable lap tray with attached crayon holder

Kids are guaranteed to love making the portable lap tray. Wherever they go, they'll enjoy taking their portable lap tray.

5.35 Toothbrush holders

Given below are the steps for making toothbrush holders:

Step 1

Pick a 2x6 scrap and let your child draw whatever shape he wants.

Printable models can be found, but it's more enjoyable for kids to be creatively independent.

Step 2

The shape is to be cut out in step 2.

You have to either do this step for your kid or extend your full support to execute this step confidently. It all depends on the age of your child. You may use jigsaw, **bandsaw**, or scroll saw. **A scroll saw** is the best tool to introduce to kids in the initial stage of their learning.

Step 3

In this step, a hole is to be drilled out on the wood's edge for the toothbrush.

You may use a one inch **Forstner bit** to drill this out. Kids usually enjoy using a drill. This step will be a lot of fun for them.

You have to ensure that everything is clamped well and correctly.

Step 4

Now is the time to apply sandpaper, which is followed by painting it with the color of your kid's choice. These activities are exciting, and kids love to carry out these tasks joyfully.

You will like the procedure followed by the kids in deciding about the type of shapes for this particular project. It gives the kids satisfaction in giving life to their creative ideas.

5.36 Banana holder

Given below are the steps for making toothbrush holders:

Step 1

Set a **compass** to 4.5 inches to make a 9-inch circle.

It will be the base of your banana holder. You may use any material of your choice and liking.

Step 2

In this step, the circle is to be cut out for the base.

The circle is not the recommended or compulsory shape for the base of a banana holder. So, you don't have to cut a circle, and can rather cut in any shape that you and your kid like.

Step 3

Then a **3/4-inch dowel is cut** for the stand.

Typically, the hand tools can help to keep your kids involved your kids in the shop. So, kids will be enjoying the use of saw in this step.

Step 4

In this step, a 3/8-inch dowel is cut for the hook.

Step 5

In this step, a hole is to be drilled in the stand at an angle that will support the 3/8" dowel hook.

You do not have to be perfect in working out the angle for this hole. Just help your child use his judgment and idea.

Step 6

In this step, a ¾ inch hole is to be drilled in the base. This hole will be used to support and hold the ¾ inch dowel stand.

Like in the previous step, you do not have to be perfect in working out the angle for this hole. Just help your child use his judgment and idea. You have to drill this hole close to the edge of the circle. Do not drill in the middle of the base.

Step 7

The time has come to glue the dowels. Gluing is a fun activity that kids like to do.

Then apply sandpaper and help your child complete his project.

5.37 Camp Folding Tripod Stool

What about making a vintage camping bench to celebrate the woods' Design Sponge concept this weekend? Have you observed, first of all, new portable tripod stools? They're gross as hell, and if you purchased

one, your grandfather would be disappointed. You'll be seated in luxury by the fireplace with the aid of a few sturdy pieces of wood, some hardware, and a bit of leather or thick canvas. The materials would also just cost you at least

about $20.

Few resources you'll require:

- The Sander

- The Drill

- Center-finder (only optional, but it helps) (optional, but helps)

- Tiny socket tool to conform to the acorn nuts

- The Screwdriver

- The knife

- The Rags

- Leather or any other robust seating fabrics

- the Three 1 1/8" hardwood dowels from Birch - sufficient for three 24" bits

- One 1.5-inch eyehole screw

- One 2.75" steel bolt - Modified, the brass is very weak for physical strain."

- Three finishing washers for brass

- Two brass metal acorn nuts

- Three washers of brass

- The finish used – You can also use Osmo Poly X-Oil

- Three 1" wood screws of brass (large enough not to slip across the finishing washer)

The directions:

1. Begin by splitting the dowels to or nearest to 24". Here 48" dowels have been used, so after the saw blade's part, every leg is around 23 8/8. Fully drill a hole in everyone, 10.5" in each leg's top." Find the middle of the peak of each leg, then hit a tiny pilot hole for the screws for bench fitting. To avoid your legs from separating, you will require the pilot hole. Brush each of the legs effortlessly, and a bit along the tops' side and a fair bit of filling it out further on every

bottom. It doesn't need to be flawless; ensure you don't do too much rounding to shorten either leg.

2. After cutting, drilling, and varnishing the legs, add the preferred finish and place it aside for drying. When they dry, you may continue working on the content of the seat. You can with leather if you have enough of it with you, but a thick canvas bench or various fabrics may be stitched together. As there would be a fair amount of strain on every corner, please ensure it is strong and adequately reinforced. You can place a tab on one side of the bench

for the holding strap, but it is extra. You can fix a closing strap to it, which is strongly recommended for using irrespective of a holding strap. In storing or holding it will prevent the stool from bursting open. You can then brush the leather parts and apply carnauba wax on the sleek surfaces.

3. Arrange the frame structure by tying two of the legs along with the screw once the legs have dried, with that eyehole screw in the center. On each side, employ washers to mount the acorn nut. With the hacksaw, cut the bolt down slightly so it fits tightly. You may require a bit of play in the structure to move, but it mustn't be gaping. Load the eye

hole screw (which can be cut down a little too) into that third leg until those two legs are stable, and connect it with the washer and the acorn nut. With the socket nut, secure all acorns tightly.

4. Use a wide fitting washer and the wood screw to connect the seat to all the legs after the framework is done. Don't excessively tighten and remove the holes off for these fixing sites. You'll require all the power. You may take a seat when everything is safe. The central bolt can bend to the pressure a bit, but that's alright, it will continuously hold its curve, and this shape will support the fold-up position. You are now

able to sit at the next campfire in distinct warmth.

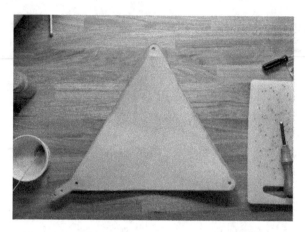

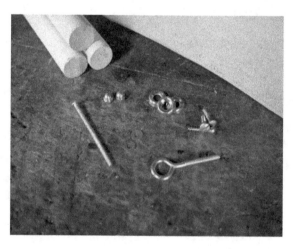

5.38 DIY new hanger for plant

For cheaper than $20, create this DIY New Flower Hanger! You can use it as a hanger for indoor plants, but you might also use it as an outdoor hanger for plants! To suit the space

and also have fun doing it, scale it down or up. It is a perfect project for newbies using wood!

If you adore plants and love the architecture of the mid-century then having only several plant hangers for the house would be interesting just a few years earlier. It is one of such tasks. You will learn to appreciate how things have worked out. It would be the best time for you to pick your materials and create a wooden hanger of plants yourself!

This idea is undoubtedly coming together in the afternoon and will not require many materials (or expertise). You might quickly apply the project panel, which can be utilized from scraps of hardwood. Be innovative and have great times doing that!

SUPPLIES OF Wooden PLANT HANGER

- The Screws (two-three inches) (2-3 inches)

- Cord/ Rope

- Solid wood Task Panel

- Dye /Stain

- The Drywall Hanger Ceiling Hooks

- The jigsaw

- Polishing block

- The Locks/Clamps

- The Drill

How to Create a DIY New Hanger for Plants

1. Choose a teardrop design. If you want, you can create a moderately big teardrop.

2. On the wood, trace the shape.

3. Bolt another block of wood with the design panel piece. Gradually cut the shape out using a jigsaw.

4. For the interior of the teardrop, repeat that tracing and carving. You ought to utilize scissors initially to trim out the center of your teardrop. Glue the wood with the paper pattern, then draw the center of that teardrop to the piece of your cut teardrop. Finally, on the teardrop's inner edge, tie the teardrop together, and utilize the jigsaw. To begin a hole on the inside, use a drill with a reasonably wide head.

5. Make the base for a plant. Create a circular foundation utilizing the remaining inside portion of the teardrop. Your Dutch oven's upper surface should be ideal for a teardrop, but you might also use every circular Design in your home to create this. With the jigsaw, trim it off.

6. For the plant framework, create a wedge. As you try to attach the plant rim's base, you will notice that it would be even more durable if it touched that teardrop on all the sides. To create a wedge that will complement the teardrop and the plant base, you can utilize your trimmed teardrop shape.

7. Fix the wedge to that teardrop utilizing screws. When you hammer in the screws, fasteners will hold it bound.

8. Utilizing screws, connect the plant foundation to the wedge.

9. Paint and sand.

10. Fasten the string and suspend it.

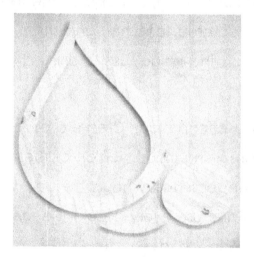

Conclusion

The urge to create something new is so much dominant in children that they fearlessly take up challenging tasks and subject themselves to any hard work to accomplish their goals. Playing with wood and tools furnishes the kids with one of the most vital skills: discipline. Children learn to get organized and disciplined in their lives. They are consequently motivated and galvanized in pursuit of fulfillment of their future life dreams. When kids go to the woodshop, they learn the skill of patience and perseverance. They comprehend the importance of these valuable skills in their life. Consequently, kids also develop subtle and gross motor expertise. They learn to coordinate hand-eye movement.

Children also develop socially and emotionally through self-assurance, accountability, self-esteem, and appreciation for supplies and safety procedures. They learn to communicate and live together in a challenging yet friendly environment. They start exploring various facts, namely size, form, distance, geometry, dimensionality, etc. They also develop engineering skills and learn the art of using their creative potential to accomplish different projects. Kids learn a range of woodworking techniques as well as various methods of playing with specific instruments. Some of the woodshops facilitate character growth. Woodworking lets children concentrate their attention on creating self-esteem such that children finish the phrase "I can't do that" daily with the term "yet."

As a woodshop is stocked with kid-sized tools, so the children are the only ones strong enough to do the right work. Tools are also even useful for the growth of children's bodies, strength, stamina, and skills. Children who have shown enough skill and concentration to use them safely can even be given power tools. The lathe can be your most popular tool for making stunning lamps and bowls with the kids.

The "tinker desk" is a spot where students will deconstruct outdated electrical gadgets and home appliances and see how they function or to find out how to repair them. Children may begin to learn the fundamentals of electronics and incorporate disassembled computer parts into their woodworking ventures. Children will create their ideas, given they will complete a project before starting another. It shows the dedication; even they are lonely or exhausted how to persevere through everything.

As kids grow up and develop their abilities, they progressively try ambitious projects. You can help kids create go-carts, tables, and benches. In a day and age where boys are disproportionately involved throughout group events such as clubs and competitive sports and absorbed in the internet and video games, it may be challenging for busy parents to create intimate interactions with their sons. If you're looking for a fun, educational, and valuable activity to do with your child, father, and son, woodworking projects are an exceptional way to get there. Knowing how to use your hands and minds to create things offers children a feeling of faith and success while giving them a full range of abilities to apply in their lives in several different ways.

It's great for kids about woodworking that you can start at a very young age. Although every infant grows differently, several tasks are suitable for fathers and sons aged five or six and up. Using the tools and performing simple tasks like early drilling and sawing helps build a lifelong hobby that feels like second nature.

CPSIA information can be obtained
at www.ICGtesting.com
Printed in the USA
BVHW061710150421
605030BV00004B/900